# CIRCLE OF HOPE

## FREDA MCEWEN

Published by Freda McEwen

Editorial Services by Heritage Editing Services

www.heritageediting.co.uk

The moral right of the author has been asserted.

# ACKNOWLEDGEMENTS

I would like to appreciate the great Lion of the tribe of Judah, my Father, for granting me the wisdom and knowledge to write this book and for being my pillar and strong tower. I salute you, Daddy.

Thanks to my earthly parents, the late Chief Fred McEwen and the Adadioranmma 1st of Agulu, Madam Esther Ozueh, for raising me to be a woman of passion who brings hope to the disheartened.

My children, Tony and Tochi Abara, for their patience and resilience in coping with my busy lifestyle.

And to my friends and well-wishers who are always with me during difficult times and in times of joy, particularly Olusola Soboyejo, Uche Adi, Amelia Nwajei, Pastor Robert,  Edwin Idehen, Ajibola Badmos and Mr and Mrs Sanni.

I am grateful to the editor of this book, Toyin Onabowu, an unassuming intellectual wiz, for her hard work. God bless you.

# About the Contributors

**Blessing Toke**

Blessing is a mother of 4 lovely kids and a registered nurse.

**Mary Urubusi**

Mary Urubusi works for the NHS as a Health Care Personnel. She has a daughter and three lovely grandchildren. She is a gospel artiste, master of ceremony, an actress who loves God very much and is extremely passionate about children's ministry.

**Sandra Mame Opokuaah**

Sandra Mame Opokuaah is a mother of 5 and an advocate for disability issues.

**Chinelo Erica Okeke**

Chinelo is a social worker, blessed with 2 children and a loving husband.

# ABOUT THE AUTHOR

**Freda McEwen (LLB, LLM, Fellow Institute Paralegal)**

Freda is a mother of two. One child is diagnosed with autism and the other a final year university student. She is involved in various community activities. She has authored three books.

# CONTENTS

# INTRODUCTION

My dear friend, please come with me to the exuberant saloon of The Uncommon Quests of Life, where I will unfold deep truths about life's journeys. I am but a guest waiting to be entertained by destiny and to, one day, say adieu for an unknown destination that I hope will be a place away from uncertainty and pain. While I am here, let me put a smile on faces beaten by tragedy.

We [the storytellers], all lovers of mankind, have exposed our misfortunes to bring hope to the hopeless. What you may consider a mess has become our message and what you might be ashamed to talk about has become our blessing to the universe. We have been through it all and come out, refined and alert warriors, conquerors, winners, and boundary breakers, unperturbed by life's drama. I do not want you to feel sorry for us but to salute life since it has given us the opportunity to stumble onto the Podium of Accomplishers, and our enemies—for propelling us to the heights of fame.

Thank you for taking time out to visit the gallery exhibits of our life experiences. You may not find all our experiences intriguing or fascinating, but please take a good look and select, for your use, any tools that will aid your passage through life's events.

# PROLOGUE

P age by page, chapter by chapter, we begin to unfold the profound truths of life's drama, by happenstance, not choice, since life has forced us to expose our dilemmas to those who care to hear.

Every interesting but different reflective account that follows is geared to impact and change the readers' lives; and the stage is set for emotional outbursts, non-judgemental comments and some stereotypical remarks.

Sometimes our gain can turn into pain—life, though unpredictable, can lure you into emotional chaos. Relax. The trip of life is one journey, and the driver ensures that you are navigated to your destination. The outcome of the trip is entirely your choice, though, and the onus is on you to either make sense of your existence or make it nonsensical.

I, for one, will indulge myself in the bowl of life's not-so-pleasantries and see how far my digestive system takes it. I would call myself an agent of contentment as I have no desire to contemplate my pains or worries, but to embrace the good things I have so far.

For the purposes of authenticity, the author recounts the following stories mostly in the words of each resilient survivor who has chosen this book as a forum to share their journey through the valley of life's hard-knocks into the light of hope.

# INTRODUCING BENJY

*A portrait of an unassuming young boy canvassed in a delicate life quest for the unanswered.*

Every expecting mum looks forward to ushering her baby into this universe, with so much optimism that the baby comes out healthy and hearty. The clock ticks, knees jerk and eyes almost pop out of heads. Everyone, not just mum, is expectant.

I will now open the gallery to exhibit the journey of a young man diagnosed with Down syndrome, and his beautiful, enchanting mum. I call her a die-hard, solid, and intelligent symbol of goodness and patience. She has come out thoroughly refined through tough experiences. Please read her story. You may have your misgivings and opinions, which is acceptable, but please step into her comfort zone as she starts her tale and unravels life's surprises.

I am sure some of us will be glued to the pages and others will be judgemental when she starts dissecting her experiences. I, for one, will take a few snapshots to add to my life gallery.

She begins her story.

Welcome to earth, Son

I remember receiving a call from the hospital telling me I had one in three chances of having a child with Down syndrome. My first reaction was laughter, as it all sounded like a joke to me. I was strongly advised to come in for an urgent further test (amniocentesis) to determine whether my foetus had Down syndrome. I refused. I refused because I was told that taking the test carried a 50% risk of losing my pregnancy. Thank God, I did not give my consent because if I had gone ahead, I would have ended up having my precious son aborted.

My pregnancy was uneventful, but I had my son prematurely at 29 weeks. At birth and throughout his stay in the Special Baby unit, no one noticed anything abnormal or identified any typical physical signs of Down syndrome. These include poor muscle tone, a short neck with excess skin folds at the back of the neck, a flattened facial profile and nose, a small head, ears and mouth, almond-shaped eyes, and a crease across the palm.

Benjy was discharged from the hospital seven weeks post-birth, but a few days before his first outpatient appointment, I noticed something unusual about the physical appearance of his eyes.

During the consultation, I mentioned my concerns to the consultant, but she did not appear perturbed by my worries. She rather reassured me that my concerns were attributable to his prematurity and protein deficiency. After a thorough assessment, however, she decided to do a chromosomal blood test to rule out Down syndrome, saying the results would take up to two weeks.

## My two-week wait

During this time, my heart was racing, beating, pounding, you name it, I experienced it all and much more.

The two-week wait for the blood test results was the longest of my life, and the limbo of anticipation was excruciating. I suddenly became very apprehensive and suffered almost all the symptoms associated with anxiety, such as sleepless nights, fatigue, racing hearts and thoughts. To worsen the experience, I suffered from hypertension.

Stepping into a dilemma

My worries, fears and concerns were not abnormal, especially when you are going through the nurturing process and developing an attachment to your baby. I jolted into action by researching Down syndrome, studying my son's appearance from head to toe and comparing his looks to the physical Down syndrome characteristics mentioned online.

Google became my companion as, day and night, I researched 'Down syndrome', two words that have come to haunt my entire being and change my life forever. Yes, it changed my whole life, but little did I know that most of the changes would be positive and not entirely as detrimental as I expected. While I was researching, I wasn't reading or seeing any positive write-ups; all I saw then were the negatives of having a child with Down syndrome. Looking back today, the reason I only noticed the negatives was that I concentrated my research on literature written by professionals, not parents of precious children with Down syndrome who are directly involved in the care of their children. The more I researched, the more depressed and miserable I became.

Eventually, after a long two weeks, I got a call from the consultant who broke what I thought then was the worst news of my life—the blood test confirmed my son had Down syndrome. That minute, my heartbeat stopped for a second then restarted at the fastest speed I have ever experienced. My world crumbled right before my eyes.

Home all alone with little Benjamin, I wept like never before with no one to console me, no one to whisper in my ears that all would be well. I sobbed uncontrollably in despair and started grieving over the normal child I wanted while Benjamin lay there, staring at me.

Reflecting on my feelings back then, I smile because things are not as bad as I envisaged. I don't blame myself for the way I felt—I am only human with so much sensitivity but, thank God, I have now gone past that stage and moved on.

## Present thought

Now I cannot imagine life without Benjamin, the energy that lights up my family and world. There is no dull moment with him, his energetic personality acts like a kick which invigorates my whole being.

## What is Down syndrome?

Down syndrome, medically known as trisomy 21, is a genetic disorder caused by the presence of an extra copy of chromosome 21[1].

---

[1] **Chromosome 21** is one of the 23 pairs of chromosomes in humans… Most people have two copies of chromosome 21, while those with three copies of chromosome 21 have Down syndrome, also called "trisomy 21" (https://en.wikipedia.org/wiki/Chromosome_21, n.d.)

This extra chromosome causes health issues such as heart defects, visual and hearing impairments, and digestive abnormalities like gastroesophageal reflux. Other problems associated with the extra chromosome are global developmental delays, behavioural problems and intellectual disability.

## Breaking the news

Sometimes I am not sure whether to say men are lucky or should I say, they are missing out on blessings and unleashed gifts? Some are wrapped up in cocoon's nests waiting to be nurtured by nature and missing out on the reality of traumas and mishaps. Others have their eyes closed in self-denial, waiting for fortune to force their eyes open.

When I broke the news of the diagnosis to my husband, he was distraught, numb and speechless. When he regained himself the following day, he told me not to disclose Benjy's diagnosis to anyone. Not even to my older kids. He believed that since Benjy did not have the looks, no one would know he had Down syndrome unless they were told. I obliged.

The torment of keeping Benjy's diagnosis secret

I walked on eggshells at home, vigilant to every comment and eavesdropping by the children.

Every day, my husband stared at Benjy, tried to convince me that he did not have the physical looks of a child with Down syndrome, and reminded me not to talk to anyone about it. He was simply in self-denial which was understandable.  I, though, had accepted Benjy's diagnosis in good faith and started loving him unconditionally.

Keeping the diagnosis secret was eating me up, and I could not keep up with it any longer, so I eventually decided to talk to my older children about it.  At this point, I had started reading about Down syndrome from parents' and individuals' perspectives, which was quite helpful as I then started seeing positive things said about people with Down syndrome.  I came across some renowned actors, models, artists, public speakers, and so on, all with Down syndrome. By the time I was ready to discuss it with my older children, I had both positive and not quite positive things to tell them about their little brother. I'm glad to say they accepted him and his diagnosis and promised to support him all the way.  That was one significant burden off my shoulder.  I was able to take a deep, relieved breath that night.

I eventually took the second bold step of talking to my close friends about the diagnosis, which made me feel freer and more comfortable.

## Benjy's Health Challenges

Just when I thought I had come to terms with Benjy's diagnosis, he started having health problems. We became regular attendants at Accident and Emergency hospital departments and paediatric wards. He suffered recurrent chest infections to the extent that he was admitted to hospital every other month, spending at least three days as an inpatient until he was four years old. Before the age of five, he had five surgeries.

Despite his health challenges, Benjy is the most amazing, energetic, friendly and caring, yet mischievous and cheeky little boy I have ever come across.

## Returning to work

After a year's maternity leave, I was struggling to decide whether to go back to work or stay at home and care for Benjy. I finally made up my mind to go back part-time and try it out for six months. If it proved more demanding than expected, I would quit.

It was challenging, as anticipated, but quitting was no longer an option when I realised my job worked as a respite and therapy for me. I always looked forward to those two days as a break from caring for Benjy, getting to meet people out there and talking about things that were totally different from Benjy and his care.

I loved caring for Benjy because no one could have done it better than me, but at the same time, I needed a break in order not to get weary or ill from exhaustion. It was not easy, though, as I sometimes had to go to work straight from the hospital. I never had annual leave because all my leave was used up for Benjy's hospital admissions. I was always exhausted—apart from Benjy's care, I had other children to look after, house chores to do, and other family commitments.

## The Sacrifice

I was eventually pushed by my circumstances into quitting my job, but I held on with my head high.  Then I started working as a community nurse two days a week and felt that was the only convenient and realistic option.  I thought I had reached a standstill in my career and could never do better.  Although somewhat anxious about the future, I made a conscious decision to take one small step at a time rather than taking a gigantic step and tumbling, and it worked for me. Over the years as Benjy's carer, I also came across carers who were thriving in caring roles and as high fliers in their professions.

## Presently

Today I can boldly say that I am doing well in my career, and Benjy and every member of my household are doing great. Having said that, the road is not smooth. No, it is still very taxing, but we have all learnt to take one step at a time with a positive attitude. We decided to persevere and remain resilient, hoping and praying good fortune would turn up on our doorstep and Benjy's creator would remember us for good.

However, I must confess that there are days when I still cry behind closed doors, not letting anyone see my little drops of tears. I also feel low and overwhelmed, sometimes, but I have never wished to exchange Benjy for anyone else.  His health is now stable, thank God, but I am still faced with his developmental challenges over which I have no say. His maker, the Great Artist, decides how to modify his art. I always pray that THE miracle will happen one day, and I will be one of those to proclaim the wonders of the maker of the universe.

Admittedly, it is hard and exhausting every day as I am faced with different challenges in supporting him to reach his developmental milestones. I have to deal with his demanding behaviours and people's negative attitudes (both young and old) towards him. But Benjy remains my special child, and I love him to the moon and back.

Looking back to when he was a premature baby and now that he is almost seven years old, I must say that Benjy has come a long way. It has been a roller coaster journey for him, our family and me, but in all things, God has been faithful.

Benjy is a very happy boy with a lovable personality. Not only is he caring and loving, he enthusiastically helps out a lot with chores. He loves cooking, and eating is his favourite hobby. He is cute and a good person at heart. Despite his condition, he finds it in his heart to love and care for others; at school, he reaches out and plays with profoundly disabled kids who are unable to join in during playtime. He gives a big hug when he senses that someone is sad because he believes little hugs here and there make everything better. Benjy is simply a fun child to have and be with.

# CHAPTER 1

## Introducing Ikechukwu

Welcome back, my friend, as I introduce you to the next portrait of a young man who has been endorsed as an overcomer. He has been through tough times and come out stronger and more able. His parents have shed tears and wept deeply, yet in every step they take, they soar in divine intervention. I invite you to go through his life's journey from birth to present. He is blessed with a supportive dad who stood against the condition to ensure that it did not destroy Mum and the baby. I will personify his condition because it is a terror, a masquerade and a puzzle whose pieces you can never put together. It lays ambush and strikes, taking its victims unaware.

If it is an ailment, it has no medical cure. If it is a disease, it is neither contagious nor infectious. If it is terminal, no one has been killed by it. Experts say it is a condition which affects communication and social interaction. It is a wide spectrum disorder; no individual is the same.

Please bear with us as we join Dad in his saloon of relief while he pours out his experiences. I am looking forward to engaging my heart in this story. You may not agree with all his views, but please allow him to engage with you.

## The birth

Nimbus clouds gathered that Saturday morning in the autumn of 2005. The wind was boisterous. It was threatening to rain. The treacherous wind had given a big blow to several trees on the streets, and they had lost most of their leaves. It was too early for such to happen since the autumn of that year had just started. The few trees that still had a lot of leaves on their branches didn't stand much chance of survival because of the strong gales.

To most people conversant with the history of the weather in the UK, the strong winds were expected. The summer of that year was very hot. Heat waves created a lot of health problems, and the Accident and Emergency section of the NHS was inundated with calls. Consequently, a very cold winter was expected to balance nature, but it came earlier than anticipated, bringing with it, sorrows, tears and blood.

In one of the wards of Lewisham Teaching Hospital, London, another type of strong autumn pressure was going on. My wife, Pamela, was in labour. She was admitted the previous night when her waters broke. Benevolent neighbours had to rush her to the hospital because I had travelled to Wales for a wedding. We were not expecting my wife to go into labour that weekend. Her EDD (the date the spontaneous onset of labour is expected to occur) was about one week ahead. When my wife rang me that Friday night, I thought she wanted to know how I was faring.

'Hero, I am in the hospital,' she said.

I became all ears to hear why.

'I'm in labour.'

I became happy and at the same time, sad that I might not be there when she put to bed. I encouraged her, and we prayed together, handing everything into God's hands.

The next morning, I took the first coach leaving for London. We set out at 6:30am, and by 9:00am, I was already in London, Victoria coach station. I quickly took a train to Lewisham, and in a jiffy, I was at the hospital where my wife was still in the labour ward. I held her hands and encouraged her. We also prayed as had been our practice. The nurses said she was not dilating properly and was under close observation. The foetus' heartbeat was also closely monitored.

I stayed with my pearl until late afternoon, but there wasn't much progress in her dilation, so I decided to quickly rush home to freshen up. I returned to the hospital at about 6pm to be informed by my wife and the doctors that they might have to carry out a caesarean on her. I objected to the idea, but my wife was in high spirits. We accepted the proposal after conferring with relations and friends who had been joining us in prayer.

At about 8pm, the doctor came in to examine my wife. After that, he said they would have to operate. The snag was that the anaesthetist was not available, but she had been contacted, and she promised to make it. By 10:30pm, I was dressed up, and we moved into the theatre, and within 15 minutes, the baby was brought out.

It was an unforgettable experience. The doctor shouted, 'it's a boy!' and handed the baby to my wife who was awake throughout the surgery. Tears of joy welled down her cheeks. I was very elated and full of joy, too. Later, they gave me the baby. He and my wife, both in very good health, were moved into the ward after my wife had spent some hours in the recovery section.

## None shall be Barren

The next morning, I started ringing up my relations to break the good news. My life had suddenly turned around for good. God had taken away our reproach of barrenness. We had been married for almost eight years before our son was born, but previous pregnancies had ended up in miscarriages. The last one was in 2004. In fact, there was a palpable fear that my wife getting pregnant again after the last one was going to be a herculean task; but God proved himself mighty, and six months after that incident, she became pregnant.

We had faced a lot of persecution from friends and relatives, and God saw us through them all. During this pregnancy, there were a lot of challenges. In fact, in one case, my wife fell down on the bus and was rushed to the A&E. After every examination, the doctors gave her and the unborn baby a clean bill of health. That was a miracle.

## The naming ceremony

As to be expected and in line with Christian tradition, on the eighth day of our son's birth, he was named. We called him Ikechukwu, an Igbo name meaning the power of God. That name was not among the names we had reserved for our baby. The new name came overnight through revelation. It was a true reflection of our love and experience with God. It has been God all through our lives since we got married.

Ikechukwu grew up daily like a good flowery plant in the spring. Everything about his childhood development was perfect. He took breast milk and drank normally. As the days passed into weeks and weeks into months, our son continued to develop healthily. As first-time parents, we did our best in following the advice of nurses, doctors and family. Our son's arrival also changed us positively. We were now looking robust.

Our joy was full.

## MMR after 12 months

When it was time for immunisation, we took our son to the surgery. Before this, I had read that the MMR vaccination (a five-dosage immunisation) had some health implications. It was said to be responsible for the rise in cases of autism in the country. We prayed and handed the whole exercise over to God. We kept all the appointments with the surgery. Apart from the usual high temperature associated with the exercise, everything went well.

Ikechukwu spurred in growth. He started crawling at six months, and by the eighth month, he was walking. He was also very handsome. Some people mistook him for a girl. He had bright eyes, a smiley face and curly hair like a girl's. Ikechukwu was the dream of every parent. Each time we went out with him, some people would make comments like: 'this child is gorgeous'. As though he understood the good comments made about him, he would always smile, showing his gapped frontal teeth, whenever he saw people.

Apart from when he was hungry, and his food was not ready, or when he wet himself when he was asleep, there were no other times that he cried over little things.

Ikechukwu was what can be described as a ' jolly good' son.

## Nurturing Ikechukwu

We showered our son, as our only child, with all the love we had. We're still giving him that.

Ikechukwu kept blossoming in his development, started talking early and soon added singing to his abilities. He was very chatty and would say ' I love mulk', a child's adulteration of the word 'milk', and ' I love Dad'. He loved watching children's television programmes on CBeebies. He also loved music, dancing and drawing, and would often drag me to my feet for us to dance around in circles. He sleeps with music even now, a lifestyle he cultivated from childhood.

We started reading him nursery rhymes and other children's books good for his age when he was very small. He loved them so much. There was a particular one titled Turters Tiny Trip. While it was being read it to him, he would pay attention to details. If I omitted a comma, he would draw my attention to it. He was always asking questions, which I saw as very good, as a Nigerian Igbo proverb states that 'anyone who knows how to ask questions will never miss his way'.

## Talent for singing

Similarly, he loved singing Christian hymns. At two years old, each time we went out on the bus or train, he would be singing Russell Carter's hymn standing on the Promises of God. When some people heard him, they marvelled. It is not a common occurrence in London where everyone minds their business. Others hated him for that. You could see it written all over their faces. Those who loved what he was doing usually encouraged us. Some prophesied that he would be a star who would take the name of God to high places. He also sang John Lennon's Imagine. Many people raised eyebrows whenever they heard him sing such a song. Non-Christians who heard him also told us he would be a pop star. We left it all in the hands of the only One who knows tomorrow.

In church, he was always lively. He would run around in gyration and jubilation. At just over two years, he could sing along to songs and choruses. One Sunday service, an usher was carried away watching him sing 'Crucified laid behind the stone, you lived to die, rejected and alone—lyrics to the song *Above All*. But the word 'crucified', he pronounced 'tootify'.

Ikechukwu was a very happy beloved child of his parents and every good-hearted person that came across him.

## Suddenly mute

One winter morning, Ikechukwu woke up crying uncontrollably. Worried, we couldn't fathom what the problem was because that was not in his nature. He rejected the food and milk offered to him. When he wanted anything, instead of speaking, he resorted to pointing and crying. Having observed that he was no longer talking and singing, we quickly booked an appointment with our local General Practitioner. After examining him, he said the situation was strange, so he recommended some therapy and made a referral to a Paediatrician.

The appointment with the paediatrician was taking so long to organise, it was like waiting for eternity. During this period, we also discovered that our son's sleep pattern had changed. He now found it difficult to sleep at night and would sometimes be awake throughout the night. In the daytime, he would only catch a nap. In some extreme cases, he wouldn't sleep at all throughout the night. That, on its own, created an atmosphere of restlessness for him and us. Sometimes, we felt really stretched, even though we took it in turns to take care of him at night. Furthermore, we noticed that his eating habits had changed, and he was now very choosy with his food. Sometimes he would eat only Weetabix or pasta, refusing every other meal.

Before this, he was in a nursery school. The new development made it hard for him to cope with other children in his class. We were always summoned to the school to pick him up because the teachers could not really understand what was happening, either. It was a traumatic time for our little boy and us, his inexperienced parents. Not long after that, the much-awaited appointment with the paediatrician was secured.

When we met with the paediatrician, we poured out our hearts to her. The elderly lady doctor listened attentively as we narrated our experiences with our son from birth to when we started noticing the changes in his behaviour. She encouraged and informed us that they would carry out their medical investigation and get back to us. We departed the clinic apprehensively, and the waiting game for the doctor's diagnosis started. We continued to pray and monitor our son's progress. As the days rolled by, things appeared to keep going contrary to our expectations.

After a few weeks, we received a letter inviting us to meet with the doctor. A few days to the date of the appointment, the hospital rang to confirm that we would be honouring the invitation. On the appointed day, we arrived early. The doctor's countenance betrayed her, even before we met with her and her team, at which point, she confirmed that they suspected autism.

There was some quiet in the room. We didn't understand what she was saying. It was as though she poured cold water on us. Suddenly Pamela, my wife, burst into tears. I joined her. We hugged each other as the doctor and her team watched.

They told us they needed to monitor the situation and create a care plan for him, but they needed our consent to their diagnosis to enable them to proceed with their plan. We refused to accept the report. We called it satanic, stressing that it wasn't for our son. The doctor said if we didn't accept their findings that they couldn't proceed with giving or recommending any care or therapy. We asked her to give us some time to let the information sink in and to think about it.

That day, our world collapsed. Pamela and I couldn't eat. We wept and asked each other questions to which we couldn't find answers. We still refused to accept the report. Later the same day, I picked up the courage to ring some of my pastor friends in Nigeria, especially those who had assisted us before and during pregnancy. They encouraged us to cooperate with the medical personnel, stressing that the diagnosis did not stop God, who works in mysterious ways, from perfecting his will. He uses difficult situations to glorify his name.

With these kind and encouraging words from family and friends, and words from the Bible, we decided to accept the doctor's diagnosis. This opened the door to another journey of life in which we all partook. Care and therapy plans were drawn up for our son, and he was referred to a school in Welling, Kent, to continue his education.

## At school

Ikechukwu made new friends and was loved by all in his new school. Every day, he looked forward to going, but on some days, it was difficult to take him to school because he did not sleep the night before. Teachers at the school were very experienced, professional and humane in their approach and attitudes. They tried to make him feel comfortable and cooperated with us, the parents, advising as needed. The school also employed a speech therapist to assist our son with regaining his speech. But as the days grew into weeks and months, none of the changes we envisaged was present.

Before this, a few days after Ikechukwu stopped talking, I saw him in my dream, playing and talking with me. I told my wife about the dream, and we prayed together, trusting God to perfect his will concerning our son. Ikechukwu lost his speech when he was three years and four months old, and we continued in prayers and strict observation of the therapies in place. On the morning of his fourth birthday, he spoke. We were overjoyed! We hugged him and started singing. He continued to make progress in his speech, but most of the time, he repeatedly used one word. He then grew into continually repeating one phrase.

When his time at the nursery was coming to an end, going to primary school became another uphill struggle. The nursery school head presented a list of schools for us to choose from, but we did not know what to do. We did not want a special school because we knew our boy copied behaviours a lot and might go into such schools and start copying children with other medical challenges. We made up our minds to send him to a mainstream school. We also felt that the best way to learn how to speak was by watching and copying others. That he could achieve in a mainstream school.

Scouting for a mainstream school where our boy would have the best of two worlds started. We visited several schools. At one school in Baxley, we were impressed with both the school and the reception the unit head gave us. It was a mission school, and we wanted a place where our son would hear God's word in addition to receiving a formal education. The head of the specialist unit said, by the grace of God, they would take care of our son. That endeared us to them, and we chose the school.  Our son joined the reception class there in September 2010. He was well received.

The school, true to their promise, did very well for him. The head of the special needs unit, a Christian lady whose son also had special needs, was superb and very motherly. She married her personal experience in the area, coupled with empathy, with her teaching experience, and gave our son the best. She was always designing new strategies to ensure that Ikechukwu had a worthwhile time at school, liaising with the appropriate agencies and multisectoral bodies whenever the need arose. She would always go into her repertoire of experience to bring out a formula that worked if one failed. Her type is very rare in a society where most people are selfish.

The unit also had a wonderful team of teachers and assistants trying their best to see that our boy and other children with special needs in the school were properly taken care of, ameliorating the pains of such challenges on the children and their parents.

## Challenging times

In the course of time, our boy was also diagnosed with ADHD, adding to our woes. He was now finding it extremely difficult to settle down both in class and at home. Sometimes, in a week, he would only go to school once or twice. It was a difficult period.

One afternoon after school, he went missing. My wife had gone to pick him up from school. Right from school, he kept insisting that he wanted to go out to play. My wife told him they needed to go home so that he could eat before they went to the park. He agreed. But when they got home, he refused to go in. Every effort to pacify him proved abortive. My wife needed to use the loo and asked him to wait at the door since he refused to enter the house. By the time she dashed back, Ikechukwu was nowhere to be found. She searched the area to no avail. She rang me, and I asked her to call the police immediately. The police arrived within five minutes, and the search for our boy began.

The officers, after interrogating her, searched our house to ensure he wasn't hiding in a wardrobe, then commenced a house to house search for Ikechukwu. They called for reinforcements and detailed them to go to the riverside near where we lived and used to take our son to play and watch birds. The concern of the officers was to ensure he didn't fall into the river and drown. Time passed quickly. When we checked, he was already missing for over 30 minutes. The search continued, and I returned to join them. After about 55 minutes, the officers received a telephone call from a lady who said she found a little boy of about five years loitering unaccompanied around a car park. The lady gave a vivid description of the child and what he was wearing that matched our son. The officers asked her to keep him and quickly instructed those at the riverside, which was near the car park, to move in swiftly.

The officers collected him, brought him to the house, sat down and started interrogating us. When they were satisfied, they left their names and advised us to be very careful, stressing that since he had gained the confidence to leave the house, the tendency to repeat that was high. They equally informed the local authority, and within a few days, letters came in the post on the subject with an appointment to visit the house. The lady who came heard our version of the story and promised that the council would put measures in place to ensure that our boy was kept busy, especially after school. That promise was kept. We also received letters from other agencies concerned with children.

Ikechukwu kept making progress in his new school. The school also put measures in place to help him to burn off excess energy. They equally facilitated appointments with medical experts and [2]CAMHS. We eventually had to move home because along with other factors, our location was no longer safe for our boy. At our new place, he went missing again, true to the police officers' prediction. He was just over seven years at the time. Thankfully, he was found at Plumstead station.

At this age, he started having ear problems. A lot of wax built up inside his ears because he wasn't allowing us to clean them and he began having seizures. Whenever they happened, he responded aggressively, punching me, his mother, or anyone around. The doctors suspected epilepsy. At this point, we were no longer worried about whatever diagnosis they came up with. All we knew was that God's will concerning our son would be done. The ear problem continued unabated, and Pamela and I kept thinking: 'why all these challenges for such a little boy?' We reposed our trust in the Lord

---

[2] Child and Adolescent Mental Health Services

who said, 'many are the afflictions of the righteous; but the Lord delivers him out of them all'(Ps 34:19 NKJV). We know that it's not beyond God's power to heal our son.

In October 2014, Ikechukwu had ear surgery in the hospital where he was born. He also had brain scans at Kings Hospital where it was established that he hadn't got epilepsy. After the ear operation, the seizures stopped, and his health and life became better. Nevertheless, he was now beginning to self-harm. The doctors said his pain threshold was low. Each time he felt a little pain, he responded to it by punching the spot, inflicting more pain on himself. During this time, he was experiencing pains on his right thigh, which the paediatrician deemed to be growing pains because he was growing too quickly. Each time he felt the pain, he would punch himself and cry. It was later discovered that a vitamin D deficiency caused the pains. That stopped with a constant dosage of vitamin D tablets.

Ever since his challenges started, Ikechukwu had constant constipation mainly due to his choice of processed foods like pasta. When he was offered vegetables, fruits or African food, he would vehemently reject them. He equally had difficulty sleeping. Whenever he wet himself, he would wake up, and going back to sleep became a herculean task. Consequently, he wore pampers to bed even at the age of nine. Even with that, sleeping was sometimes very difficult. Throughout this time, he was on Melatonin, a prescription sleeping pill, and later placed on Circadian when the former was no longer effective.

But the problem wasn't solved. Instead, we noticed some side effects. At six years of age, our boy developed pubic hairs. When we challenged the consultant who prescribed Melatonin, he claimed it wasn't the cause, even though the contraindications on the drug noted that it could lead to that. It was even observed that Melatonin wasn't licensed to be used for long periods. It was meant to be used in small doses, but our boy was left on it for years. Medical negligence causes taxpayers and families a lot of money, as well as psychological and emotional distress.

Despite all the sleeping pills, sleep was still a big issue for our son. To compound matters, Ikechukwu had resorted to not only attacking us but punching his own eyes whenever he couldn't get to sleep. We became very afraid that in brutalising himself, he could go blind. We tried all we could to restrain him, to no avail.

In the course of this, he went missing again. My mobile telephone rang, and my wife told me Ikechukwu was gone.

'What happened?' I asked.

'I was getting dressed, ready to take him out, but when I got downstairs, the door was open, and he was gone.'

I quickly dashed out to meet her. We immediately informed the police, and it didn't take long before they arrived. Before then, I started walking towards Woolwich Square because I sometimes took him down there to play. Instead of taking the bus, I walked, in case I could spot him on the road. I searched around, but our boy was nowhere to be found. My wife was also searching with the police around Lakedale Road in Plumstead, where we lived. I was confused and frustrated, asking myself when this problem would come to an end. *When would I be able to sleep with both eyes closed?*

Suddenly, my phone rang again. It was one of our church elders. I had called the presiding elder to intimate him of our predicament and solicit for prayer support. When that call came through, I thought it was to strengthen me.

'Where is your son?' The elder asked.

I told him Ikechukwu was missing and I was out looking for him.

'Where are you?' He asked again.

'At Woolwich Square.'

'Your son is with me.' He finally said.

I didn't bother to ask how or where he found him. Instead, I rushed down to the school where he worked. When I arrived, he took me to see my son who was eating crisps and having a drink. When he saw me, Ikechukwu didn't even behave as though anything was wrong.

The elder explained that one of my son's Sunday school teachers found him at a bus stop on Plumstead High Road. He asked where I was and Ikechukwu said my wife and I were at home.

'Who's here with you, then?' He asked. My son replied that he was alone, so the teacher brought him to the elder's office which was nearby.

Before I arrived, I telephoned to give my wife the good news, so she and the police officers drove down to the office where they found our boy in good condition. When they were through with interviewing the elder, they took us home and started our own interview. Once they were satisfied with our responses, they left, promising to inform Social Services as is the standard. Social Services continued from where the police stopped. Since then, we have been more cautious with Ikechukwu, and even though he now has a greater sense of the dangers of running off, we don't give him much room to do so.

Ikechukwu has continued to make progress. He's currently in secondary school, growing in stature, wisdom and favour. We're confident that the good God who created him has better plans for him. Like He said in Romans 8:28, '...and we know that in all things God works for the good of those who love him, who have been called according to his purpose'. We're optimistic that every difficulty we have faced shall turn out for our good in Jesus' mighty name.

## Presently

Ikechukwu is doing well academically, and we are optimistic that he will one day excel and get a degree. It has not been easy caring for him, and we still cry and sometimes ask why this has happened to us. It's hard to fathom that a tiny slim young man of 12 years can attack both his parents, but that has been our experience.

Autism brings out the worst in most people in a way that makes you begin to doubt your sanity. It is fearless and lawless, moving into homes uninvited and taking over their peace and tranquillity.

## We still have hope

We have been schooled by life's painful events and certificated, refined and fortified by heaven. I doff my hat to parents with children diagnosed with autism, for being the best parents ever. They are tough and resilient. I also applaud those giving a helping hand for their kindness. I have wept until I can weep no more, because we threw down a challenge to our opponent, autism, and have noticed that it is a coward that carefully chooses where to pitch its tent. As far as we are concerned, though, we are undefeated and unperturbed.

Every day, we become stronger as we learn new tactics on how to defeat this enemy. Autism creatively comes up with new ways to inflict pain, but we are overcomers. Family friends who have older children in similar situations often advise us on some positive behavioural support which has been helpful. We can also see a huge improvement in Ikechukwu's cognitive ability as we give him extra lessons at home.

Amidst all the trouble and pain, we try to be hopeful. We can see a bright light at the end of the tunnel, and we are gradually walking down that path. Do not give up, my friend. The living has hope and can explore options. Try to stay healthy and keep exploring, and *voila!* One day your answer will appear. That's the little French I know.

*Weeping may endure for a night, but joy comes in the morning (Ps 30:5).*

Stay happy.

# CHAPTER 2

## Another life tale

The beauty of existence is when you keep hearing stories that can put a smile on your face, although nobody thinks of this when unfortunate situations come knocking. I am perplexed by life events because the more I look, the less I see. Some people stumble into wealth without hard work; others work like elephants and eat like ants, and still, others work like ants and eat like elephants. We cannot choose our families, but we can decide who to befriend.

This is the story of a great woman of God, whom I respect. She is blessed with an angelic voice and the mannerisms of a lamb. Born into a family where safeguarding was non-existent, she was abused, neglected, and abandoned to fend for the family at an age when children her age were still being assisted with their personal care.

Her life took a bitter and debilitating twist from the outset, but I'll let her tell you her story in her own words.

## My aunt

I was just three years old when I found myself living with a strange woman I called Aunty. The woman with whom I lived before was a very good woman who treated me like a princess. People in this new family were horrible and nasty to me. The wickedness and inhuman treatment I faced was unconscionable, to the extent that I received no treatment when I contracted chicken pox. It was as though I was an enemy or the source of all their misfortunes. My aunt was childless, and perhaps that was why she did not know how to treat me.

My mother gave me to my aunt to care for me, but she never did. Although she enrolled me in school, I never did well because I would often miss school or be engaged in house chores.

## The treatment

You cannot begin to imagine how awfully my aunt treated me. Recalling my experiences is like digging a sword into my chest. She beat me with a stick countless times for being alive. I can only assume my presence reminded her of her childlessness and she would do anything to see me disappear.

Pain became my companion. I washed clothes like a washerwoman from a tender age, constantly drenched in sweat, often drinking the salty fluid from my nostrils. My delicate skin was scorched with blisters from the sun as, with my aunt's permission, I hawked for over twenty miles each day for my uncle's second wife.

I faced all kinds of humiliating circumstances as men with their obscene and lascivious nature paraded around me like flies, dragging me into secret corners to have their wicked way with me under the pretext of buying goods for which they never paid me. I cannot remember how often I was repeatedly raped by men old enough to be my grandfather.

It was painful and humiliating, and I could only helplessly observe the animalistic nature of those demonic men as they pressed their rough bodies against me. It was like visiting hell alive. I was a virgin, a primary school girl with a delicate hymen. What did such men gain from penetrating a child? It was disgusting and evil. I cursed them from their mother's womb every time they raped me. They shamelessly took my life and my womanhood from me.

Family or foe?

This is the question I kept asking at an early age after experiencing all kinds of abuse, the icing on which cake was sexual abuse. The family meant to safeguard and protect me suddenly exposed me to risks which resulted in my being endangered as wild animals in human form molested me. As though the appalling treatment I received was not enough, we went to church one day where someone—who I won't name here—inserted ground pepper into my private parts as punishment because they suspected that I was sleeping around!

My mum's sister repeatedly told me I would never amount to anything, showing how much, she hated me, and that for no reason. However, as the Good Book says, 'a causeless curse will not come or alight'[3]. Her words actually gave me the confidence to move forward.

The angel came by

---

[3] Paraphrased from Proverbs 26:2

I eventually decided to write a letter to the angelic woman I lived with before I moved to this hell. I could not fill her in on the extent of the vile treatment I received, but I appealed to her for help.

The woman received my letter and paid us a visit. She was very kind and approachable, and for the first time I was treated like a person and listened to. Permit me to say that Africans struggle to show kindness to any child who is not their blood, but this lady[*4] registered me in a primary school. I finished and went on to secondary school as a boarder where, for the first time, I started enjoying school and making friends. Life was becoming more meaningful and worth living.

After I finished my secondary school education, I started my acting and singing career and immersed my whole being into ensuring that I succeeded, regardless of what it took. I grew up to be very attractive and decided to capitalise on my physical attributes. With a lot of hard work, I was able to start a modelling career. Life's fortunes wiped my tears away, and I never wept again. A few years later, I moved to the United Kingdom, continued pursuing my singing career, and I soon recorded my first album.

I subsequently gave birth to a beautiful baby girl whose life exceeded all my expectations for her. She attended University, got a good job, married at the right age and gave me grandchildren.

---

[4] It wasn't until much later that I discovered that my angel was actually my birth mother! She had agreed to my childless aunt's request for me to live with her but had no idea how much I was being ill-treated.

# Married

Finally, after having a child out of wedlock, the good Lord remembered me.

I went to Africa to get married to a man my sister introduced to me. I thought the man was a blessing that came to me at the right time. But no, my friend, the man was so nasty that when I got pregnant and miscarried the baby, he left me to get on with my pain and never even came to see me at the hospital.

I was heart-broken. I had been looking forward to having another child. The man in question was also having extramarital affairs, so I eventually had to say goodbye and close the chapter of heartbreak. What would have become of me if I had remained with this man?

# At present

We are here today, and tomorrow we are gone. I laugh at people who decide to avoid their past but keep making the same mistakes. Some men marry another woman because their wife has a disabled child. What makes them think the child with the new spouse will be void of disability? As if we have an ultimate say. Life is not a tick box exercise; you cannot say an older woman will have a down syndrome baby. These days, so do young people. The fact that you are ill does not mean you will die, but healthy people die, too. Being very careful and only eating organic food does not make you immune to sickness. Some reckless people live to be 100 years old.

Where you are today is not just by your will or works, but often by divine ordination and intervention.

I have been embittered by life's events and battered by the trauma of simply existing in this universe. It has not been an easy journey, but thankfully, God, my energiser, helped me bulldoze past all the traumatic experiences. I was shattered, but he divinely picked up all the pieces, put them together carefully, and placed me back in his art gallery to be exhibited as one of his masterpieces. Thank God that no man has the final say about where and when life can take us.

I am truly enjoying my life with a good job, a mortgage and a music career.  I am indeed a walking blessing, well looked after by the God of the universe. I stand forever grateful to him.

# CHAPTER 3

## Another intriguing story

I am now going to invite you to look closely at the portrait of a black, lustrous, enticing and dazzling African beauty. She is the mother of **Jonathan** who was once delicately encased in the walls of her womb and eventually ushered into this unassuming woman's bosom where he found refuge from a distastefully callous world. This is her account of her experience.

## The birth

Jonathan is the fourth-born of his siblings. Everything was fine before his birth. I was healthy and craved charcoal and okra with plantain every morning. I put on a lot of weight. Because I had a history of deep vein thrombosis, I was injected with Heparin throughout the pregnancy and for six weeks afterwards to prevent blood clots.

I was at home when the contractions kicked in, and the labour started normally. Once I arrived at the hospital, I was prepared for labour and, within two hours, the baby arrived with no complications.

## Baby development

Jonathan was a big baby and ate a lot. As he grew, he was diagnosed with eczema for his dry skin, but he was a very active and happy baby. He walked at 11 months and, around 15 months, started saying words like dada, mama, as well as his siblings' names. Nothing unusual was detected. There was a debate about the MMR jab at the time, and everybody was waiting to see if the then Prime Minister, Tony Blair, would give the same to his son. I was a little worried about my son receiving it, but I was also concerned about the potential complications if he didn't. I didn't know anything about single jabs, but after long consideration, I went ahead and allowed him to have the injection.

## Onset of Autism

Jonathan met the milestones expected of a child his age. I was happily looking forward to enjoying my motherhood, not realising I would soon be visited by some uncertainties.

> When you are rejoicing over something, be hopeful that it will last forever. Sometimes, we are scared of inevitable things, but the only unavoidable thing is death. Autism can be managed.

About four weeks after receiving the MMR jab, Jonathan started showing withdrawal symptoms and would not answer to his name. We initially thought he had a hearing problem and ask the GP for a referral to the hospital. That test came back negative—nothing was wrong with Jonathan, yet he still ignored any conversations. He was then referred to a paediatrician and finally seen after six months. Every attempt to do the test was unsuccessful, he would not respond to anything but kept crying with a very high-pitched voice, hitting his head with his hands and against the wall.

I am not sure why people with autism decide to be selectively mute, but I do not blame them. The world is so full of noise that comes from everywhere no matter how hard you try to block it out. I do think I am beginning to understand the sudden shut down in communication; or perhaps not, since, the more answers I seek, the more hopeless the situation appears.

## The diagnosis and the shame

Then the news I didn't want to hear finally arrived. My son had autism.

I had no clue what it was and very distraught. I wallowed in self-denial for a couple of months, while his dad became a stranger, a different person from the man I married. The shame of having a child with special needs soon overshadowed our once loving family. The chill and tranquillity had been replaced with a gruesome, pervasive sadness. Everyone walked on eggshells to avoid my husband as he barked at everyone and everything in sight, but my focus was on smothering my new baby with love and care.

It was time to point fingers—who was to blame for this strange ailment? Whose family did it run in? Mine or my husband's? There was no point in pondering on the answers to these questions. From my experience as an African, a child's negative traits are the mother's fault, and if it is positive, it is inherited from Dad.

I raise my hand in acceptance, it is my fault since the baby came from me.

## Autism, the puzzle

I was left to deal with finding out more about this condition called Autism.  I attended programmes and courses that were available to me. I began to question whether it was something I had done, wondering if I was living under a curse and who might have cursed me. I had struggled in previous relationships and was glad to be happily married after suffering many hurts and abuse from family and past partners. I thought fortune had put a smile on my face this time, but no, a new chapter of pain had opened up.

This was my husband's first child, and his family started making hurtful comments about my sick son. I became the main source of family entertainment, every family gathering had my name as the main course, my son as the appetiser and his condition as dessert. His siblings also had to deal with friends making remarks about him, but they learned to cope well along the way.

Jonathan started being aggressive and displaying very challenging behaviours. We couldn't go out without strapping him in a buggy, and even then, people stared at me as though I was a bad mum. I later became pregnant with his brother, and that was extra difficult, as Jonathan drained me of all energy. By this time, it had been three years since he last spoke, and I could not get him into a nursery.

# The Sacrifice: short-changed by life

I had to give up my full-time job as a dental nurse to offer Jonathan full support and learn more about his condition. I started to eliminate certain foods and cook only organic meals for him, not caring about the cost. I simply wanted my son to get better.

# The praying mum

Even though I prayed over and anointed him every day, my hope sometimes dwindled. But I kept going, not knowing if God heard me. Family members could not cope with my son being around, and it was hard to enjoy any outings, including church, but I kept going and even travelled with him.

# Interrogating destiny

Jonathan's condition became more and more demanding. I felt trapped and unable to focus on anything meaningful as the situation consumed my whole being. It was as though I suddenly stopped breathing and was gradually diminishing.

I struggled to take him on holidays. No one wanted to sit next to us on the plane, and they kept staring at us at the airport.

Autism demonstrates the arrogant and demonic side of people, which I experienced in the way I was ill-treated in my country. People looked at us with disgust as though we were objects of ridicule. Some even went as far as calling him both naughty and demon possessed, to our horror.

# Spiritual encounter/revelation

One day, when I was praying for Jonathan, the Holy Spirit led me to John 9, where Jesus talked about the blind young man. His blindness was not because he or his parents had sinned, but it happened so that God's power would be demonstrated. This gave me comfort and a new meaning to my purpose as Jonathan's mother. I was now that proud, very excited and unashamed mum.

## Marital breakdown

Disability is not to be trifled with; Autism is not a physical or mental illness. It is difficult to know where it comes from or where it is going. It is like a chameleon that changes colour.

Unfortunately, my husband and I split up, which had a devastating effect on me. I would never have imagined a father leaving his disabled child behind, or for me to cope with on my own.

We eventually moved churches, and my new pastor was very understanding. His wife also gave me an opportunity, during a church service, to explain my son's condition to the church. It was the first time that I didn't witness any person's attempt to perform a deliverance on my son because he was demon possessed. Instead, the word of God that came to me daily gave me hope and strength.

I felt bitter and neglected many times, but God has seen us through. As Jonathan was growing up, I began studying again and taking care of his four siblings, while doing just about any work to keep us going. I subsequently returned to my career but found it unfulfilling, so I went back to University to study healthcare. I knew my experiences could help others, particularly those who felt isolated, don't go to church, or out at all.

Jonathan eventually spoke when he was almost 10 years old, and he is now almost 18. We've come a long way, but God has been good. We are still going strong and have been a blessing to many families over the years, encouraging them to accept and manage this condition.

## At present

I am content and fulfilled. I am accomplishing all that God intends for my life and have just graduated from University with a degree that will enable me to touch the lives of women like myself. My daughter is married and expecting a baby. I am as happy as can be, with no qualms about what the future holds. I am under the auspices of the One who created me and has a say in my existence.

## Finale from Jonathan's mum

I always tell other parents to be FOCUSED>> DEDICATED>>> BUT HAVE NO EXPECTATIONS.

This way, you don't give up when nothing is happening, but you continue to pursue and get all the support and education to help your child develop. God will surprise you when you least expect it because you had no expectations of your own. When you have expectations, you give up easily, but when you don't, you continue no matter what comes your way. Autism is not A CURSE! See it as your ministry to create awareness for others.

GOD BLESS!

# CHAPTER 4

## Introducing Chisimdi

Please come with me to take a glance at the portrait of Chisimdi's mum, an adorable woman of virtue and enchanting masterpiece, and her long-awaited gift of the womb.

## Painful but hopeful

Time slows down when you are preoccupied with the cares of this world, and it did crawl at some point in my life. I was a shadow of a person so bamboozled by a life tragedy that I eloped into a world of isolation where I felt overwhelmed by anxiety. I felt mashed up within and without, having had three stillbirths before the age of 24. It was as though I was not woman enough to carry a baby to full-term. I was tossed around by life and mimicked by my inner turmoil.

I was lucky or, more aptly, blessed to be loved by a selfless man who knew the true meaning of 'for better or worse' and ignored all the voices of reproach. He did not concentrate on our present situation but was hopeful that life would take a positive turn. Clothed with shame and pity for my husband who had to mourn the children with me, I felt I did not deserve his love and concern. He was only worried about my worries. He showered me with more love and care, and the more he did it, the more I felt I betrayed him. I wet my pillow and his arms that cuddled me every night with tears. I prayed, fasted, and meditated but to no avail. Nothing seemed to be working except my tear ducts.

## Suggestions!

Suggestions, these I never lacked, but they were all irrelevant and destructive. People tagged me with all kinds of oppressive spiritual problems. I became a toy in the hands of pastors who felt they had answers to the chaos in my life; but what they attempted created more chaos and self-blame. Health professionals gave up on me and waited for the next stillbirth to occur. Without remorse, they pre-empted my pain and shattered my faith. The whole issue took a toll on me, and I was blackmailed by idealism, as nature refused to embrace me.

When I came to the United Kingdom with my husband, I thought the health care system would play a role in rewriting my destiny. Perhaps they would find the hidden answers to my years of worries and agony. No, they had no solution, and once again I buried another baby. That is my plight, my friend. My pain continued, and I was again taken advantage of by people who felt they had spiritual answers.

I waited and hoped things would change in my life, though within me, I was hopeless. There seemed to be no light at the end of the tunnel, only a dark, hideous path waiting for me to walk past and be devoured.

The love of my life, my dear husband, was still unperturbed. He was an onlooker who refused to be diminished by life's commotions.

He continued loving and caring for me. He never considered having babies as one of life's requirements or proof of an adequate existence. He saw babies as gifts given to mankind when the time is ripe and felt I was impatient and self-reliant. I needed to take time out to dwell on positive thoughts that would help me become whole again. I had saturated myself with ugly, negative thoughts as though that was the answer to my problem. No, they were contributory factors to my sorrow.

You could not imagine my pain unless you were to walk in my shoes, which I pray you don't. Carrying a deceased baby in my arms was unbecoming for any woman, and the pain I bore at my delicate tender age was unfair. I did everything I was expected to do-including getting married at the right time and in the right way. But my predicament was not about my good works but about the events nature planned for my life. At that point, I wished that life's schedule would take a different turn. *Surely it must at some point?*

My husband kept encouraging me to be strong, determined not to be a pushover and to get my life back. I am the creator of my pain and joy since it is up to me to make those choices. I was interested in people's opinions about my situation, which was all my assumptions, nothing concrete. My husband constantly reassured me that it was about us and no one else. Children would come and leave when they are old enough, but we will always have each other. They might even decide to put us in care homes or abandon us in our old age. We don't know what tomorrow holds.

I was beginning to lose count of my stillbirth pregnancies and babies that died days after delivery. My hope was becoming non-existent as the years progressed.

## Processing my internalised depression

After a while of processing my pain, I decided to search out answers and solutions. I reflected on where my life started in clay form before I was transformed into a human being. I was empty from the outset and had no say as to what form I would take.

It was up to the sculptor to transform me into whatever creature or sex he pleased, and he chose **woman**, a child bearer. It was time to throw in the towel and allow him to take over. I was nothing until he made me something, yet he could have allowed me to remain in the state of dust. Dust that we brush off our furniture may be unsculptured human beings or those who have been human and returned to dust. What is flesh that we are so consumed by it?

As I retraced my steps to where this journey of pain started, some people told me I married the wrong man, some that I had a spiritual husband, and others blamed my birth mother. The journey taught me so much about life. I had internalised depression over the years and can only thank God that I did not develop mental health problems. I relaxed and waited for God to decide. He meant well for me, but I had been too faithless.

My life journey took a new turn as I swapped hopelessness for hope and resilience, immersed myself in the spirit of contentment, and received reassurance.

This time I became pregnant and flew to Ireland to have my baby. I was hopeful that there would be no more burials, no more pains. Joy and excitement rekindled inside me. On the delivery day, I was excited and certain this baby would come out with no qualms. Everyone was anxious and eager to hear and see the outcome. I went into labour and went to the National Maternity Hospital where the doctor ran a quick check on me and told me to go home because the baby was not forthcoming. My husband pleaded with the doctor to admit me to the hospital so I could be properly monitored since I had previously lost my babies in Nigeria, but the doctors refused, stating that the hospital was not a hotel.

We left, and two days later I went into labour, but this time, the baby had stopped moving. We arrived at the hospital and after a scan to ascertain the position of the baby, the doctors noted that the baby's organs had failed. Because I had eaten a few hours before the scan, I had to wait for hours to be operated on. I felt the baby come out of me motionless.

Still, lifeless and stiff he had returned to where he came from within two days. This was not my decision; the artist decides which gallery to place the art in and it was not mine at that moment. He chose to take him back, perhaps he had unfinished work with him and did not want me to suffer. I held my handsome but swollen and stiff son in my arms. The experience gave birth to the reality of the human existence, and I was no longer in self–denial of the fact that I am but a piece of artwork.

I cried until there were no tears left. My husband also cried like a baby beside me, even as he assured me that our journey was not over yet. The health professionals looked on sympathetically, but that was nothing at that point.

'You need to stop now before you kill yourself.' My husband suddenly said in a low voice. 'Why don't we adopt a child?'

I looked at him in dismay and felt he was patronising me as though I was not woman enough to deliver a living baby.

The drama that played out during that period unveiled a stage-managed episode of his family offering him another woman who could achieve this. I felt inadequate for a while. My friend, that was not the case, the man never changed his attitude towards me. Like I said, he is one in a million, a man of action and few words. He is very realistic about life and was not dissuaded by my emotional outbursts. He did not allow my dampened spirit to contaminate his inner strength. Knowing the solution would come one day, he chose not to speed up the process but allow it to come whenever it chose.

> The race is not always to the swift,
> Nor the battle to the strong,
> Nor satisfaction to the wise,
> Nor riches to the smart,
> Nor grace to the learned.
> Time and chance happen to them all[5].

---

[5] Partially quoted from Ecclesiastes 9:11

## My diagnosis

Towards the end of 2002, I fell pregnant again and, this time, was referred to King's College Hospital, but the doctors there had no insight into what the problem was and could not arrive at anything conclusive. They called it all sorts of names such as thalassaemia, but the bottom line was, it was something to do with anaemia that fell into the one percentile 'inexplicable' category. They decided it might be a severe case of thalassaemia, a condition that can affect the baby's organs, and labelled me the lady with the unknown anaemia. The doctors confirmed that it had nothing to do with antibodies because I was not producing any. I am Rhesus negative, and my husband is Rh positive, it was nothing to do with Rs negative either since my blood group is O negative and my husband is O positive.

The doctors stated my baby would not live beyond two years, and even if she did, she would be blood dependent for life. Taking a gamble with the situation, they decided that the only way to keep my babies alive from that point on until birth was through an inter-uterine blood transfusion to give them blood while still in the womb. They also recommended a bone marrow transplant at birth.

## The inter-uterine blood transfusion

The process required a long needle to be passed through my belly to the baby and then transfuse blood. A painful procedure that carries the risk of infection and miscarriage, it is monitored through a scan which enables you to observe everything. During the transfusion, they punctured an umbilical cord, and my daughter started bleeding. The doctor immediately removed the needle and said that to save her life, he was going to give her blood in her heart, with a dire warning that if I moved the baby would die. I forced myself to be as still as a statue until the procedure was concluded. I wanted a child badly and couldn't bear anything happening to this one. He placed the needle in her heart and gave her blood, but her heart stopped beating immediately. Mine would have stopped, but for the still small voice's soothing assurance and, thankfully, the baby came back to life after a few minutes.

To the doctors, it was still a hopeless case, and I was told to prepare my mind for the worst–that she could die within a few days, although an elective C-Section was planned to deliver the baby at seven months.

I subsequently lost yet another child through the same procedure because of a puncture that resulted in her losing a lot of blood. The doctors took me in for a Caesarean, and the baby came out like a vegetable, which meant she would never walk or live normally. She died a few minutes after delivery.

## The dreamer

At this point, a friend called to say she dreamt I had a baby girl but was confused as to why the baby looked very skinny in the dream. I felt she was talking nonsense—I had been told by renowned pastors and men of God that I was having a baby boy. My friend insisted that her dreams usually came to pass, but I ignored her.

That week, I went for my ultrasound, and the lady confirmed that I was carrying a girl. The doctor suggested a blood transfusion because the baby was anaemic, but that termination was probably a better option. My husband decided we had to listen to the doctor and terminate the pregnancy. I was confused and torn between my motherly instincts and the professional advice. In my confusion that morning, I contemplated terminating the pregnancy. I called my dreamer friend to fill her in on our intentions.

'Don't do it!' She pleaded. 'Please don't terminate the pregnancy. Have the baby for me—I will raise her, no matter what state she's in!' She continued.

I couldn't think straight to give her a coherent answer, but she kept insisting that I should keep the pregnancy. After a while, it was as though I gave birth to hope, so I stood my ground and told the doctor and my husband that I was keeping the baby.

My husband's concern was that he did not want anything bad to happen to me, or for me to raise a child with a disability. He knew my limitations: it would take its toll on me, and I would not be able to cope, but he eventually decided to let me do what I wanted.

I prayerfully carried the baby to term with the support of my husband, family and the dreamer who consistently encouraged me with prayers and words of wisdom. I was fearful but reassured that nothing bad would happen anymore. I was so fearful and tearful on the day of the final scan, unsure what to expect. This was my last stop—after this pregnancy, I would either adopt or go for surrogacy.

# The birth

My dear, I did not do either—adoption or surrogacy--but had my baby without any complications. She came out of my womb crying, which was a good sign. I had never heard a baby cry from my previous pregnancies. She came out boisterous and agile with no intimidation by any negative force. At that point, I knew hope had just walked in, and I should embrace it. So, I did.

The doctor was bemused, and my husband was disorientated. 'Darling, I'm sorry,' was all he kept saying. He did not know what else to do or say. It was not his fault, he had been adhering to professional advice.

I was filled with unspeakable joy and hope when Chisimdi, my angel, was handed to me. She was lovely and unassuming, just as pictured by the dreamer. She was monitored for 10 days before being discharged, and the doctors insisted she should be followed up for a year, during which she must not leave the UK.

I am glad I was chosen to receive an uncommon blessing and reward from God. It is never too late. My husband and I are not perfect, but we were chosen to receive an extraordinary spiritual advantage. The dreamer was not a saint but a willing instrument to carry out the task. She had compassion, sincerity and unconditional love for me without requiring any material gratification. God chooses who he feels could carry out a task and sends them. He is all-knowing.

If God decrees it, it happens. If it does not happen, he never said it. He is no respecter of persons and will not speak to please you. He speaks what he wants to happen, and does not waste time with empty talk., What he says is full of life and expectation.

## My husband, my children and I at present

We are doing wonderfully well. I later gave birth to a son, Chinedu. Chisimdi, my daughter, had four blood transfusions before birth while her brother had six. She is now fourteen, has passed her 11 plus exams and attends Rochester Grammar School in Kent, and my ten-year-old son attends one of the best primary schools in Kent. He is looking forward to taking his 11+ exams next September. They are both very bright and intelligent. Neither has needed a blood transfusion till date.

**We Thank God.**

# CHAPTER 5

## Being candid

When people decide to mess up your life, don't let them. Take a walk or deal with the situation.

When people decide to go, let them. You are not joined at the hip. Even Siamese twins decide to be disjointed. Do not fight to be with a man or woman, you may be taking in what God has removed for your own good. No one is responsible for your pain. Not even your birth mum—she is human with so many imperfections that only the Creator can perfect. Learn from her mistakes and move on. When your husband or wife refuses to show you love, do not get depressed and see them as wicked. They may not have known or experienced love, either, and you cannot share what is not in your possession. Do not be self-centred—teach them how to love by demonstration. If they do not reciprocate, they are not cut out to love.

People get depressed because they look at what they do not have and forget about what they do possess. Life is not a bed of roses and a place for laughter 24 hours, 7 days a week. It is full of uncertainties, and we need to be mindful of that. People drown themselves in alcohol because they want to numb some ugly life circumstances, but they wake up afterwards, exactly where they were before, hopeless and helpless.

When you feel you cannot cope with a situation, look at people who have been through the same journey and study their coping mechanisms.

## A special word to our friends who are living with autism

Please try to take enough respite to cool your head from managing the symptoms of autism. Your child may not be completely normal, but his condition can be managed effectively. Look at the communication needs of your child and learn how to deal with them. If you can get this right, you are halfway there. Please explore the various strategies available.

Also, pay attention to your child's sensory needs. It is very important to teach him or her to self-regulate her emotions. Overall, do not concentrate so much on cognitive ability as most people with autism are geniuses debarred by sensory and communication needs. They are alert, intellectual wizards waiting to be celebrated.

## A word from the author

We are the creators of our own destiny and expectations. We have the power to thwart or cut them short. People around us can influence our lives, and the company we keep can propel us to heights of self-actualisation or the lowest hierarchy in an endless attempt to meet our physiological needs. If the company you keep do not challenge you, they are not right for you.

Many of us are perturbed by people's opinions of us, which is why we are men-pleasers, always looking around for people to evaluate us. My friend, you have no business doing that. Seek the approval of the only One who never sleeps and watches over you 24 hours of the day; who stays when everyone goes, wipes your tears when no one cares, cuddles you to His bosom when you are at the verge of sanity, and saturates you with peace. He loves you unconditionally. Even during your naughty days, He overlooks your imperfections and commends your perfections, always optimistic about all your endeavours.

What is life that you are so consumed by acquisition? You are but a tool in the hand of the owner who uses you as he pleases. Don't think you have a say as to where your life goes and comes; you may know where this second but be clueless the next. Why not accept your position on this earth and be hopeful and joyful?

Do not compare yourself to other people. You are unique, and your life is specifically planned and tailored. Most of us have ignored this, sought ways to rewrite our future and ended up with pains and sorrows. You are not me or anyone else, so learn to be you. Walk with boldness and contentment. You are neither a mistake nor born to be a failure. Concentrate on finding out who you are and where life is driving you to. Do not be envious of others, do not be covetous. Learn to love yourself, and you will never ever be disappointed.

All your answers lie within; listen to that inner voice, and you will never be led astray. Chill, my friend, in the comfort of you, to find peace and tranquillity. The artist who created you made a masterpiece. You are one in a million—there is no replication in life's gallery.  Be happy because you can definitely choose your emotional state. As for me, I love myself and do not wish to be any other person. I am content and consumed with being me. You cannot give what you do not have or love me if you do not love yourself.

The gallery of life is open, and everyone is taking a glance at every piece. One of those unique canvasses showcases all that is in you, so be bold because you have a lot to offer and live for. Let your hair down, inhale the beautiful fresh air and exude inner peace. Live as though nothing is holding you back; really nothing is but you. I speak as one who has faced life's challenges and come out stronger, wiser and bolder.  I am like an animal facing the firing squad, chewing gum, with its legs crossed. I am not looking for a pity party but for people who will push me to become what I am destined to be: an overcomer, prosperous and unlimited by life.

## Grand finale

My dear friend, thanks for going through our journal and dissecting some of our life experiences. I hope you have found some answers, grasped some coping mechanisms and are ready to live life to its fullest.